Every Door Thrown Open

Every Door Thrown Open

Poems

Barbara Ford

© 2025 Barbara Ford. All rights reserved.
This material may not be reproduced in any form, published,
reprinted, recorded, performed, broadcast,
rewritten, or redistributed without
the explicit permission of Barbara Ford.
All such actions are strictly prohibited by law.

Cover design by Shay Culligan
Cover image "Stepping into the Light"
by Padgett McFeely
Author photo by Kit Hedman

ISBN: 978-1-63980-991-2

Kelsay Books
502 South 1040 East, A-119
American Fork, Utah 84003
Kelsaybooks.com

*for Terry and Mimi,
my Leos*

Acknowledgments

Many thanks to these journals and publications for publishing the following poems, some in earlier versions:

Chaparral Poetry Forum Journal: "Spell for Finding"
Colorado Central: "Patience," "Absolution"
Desert Call: "Pilgrim"
Encore: "The Smoke Break"
Lilliput Review: "how the past retreats"
Pilgrimage: "Jamais Vu"
Quartet: "Interior with Ida in a White Chair"
San Juan Independent, Heard of Poets: "Fault Lines"

"Spinster," "Tips for Living in an Occupied Country," and "Last Rothko" first appeared in *In Pursuit of Happenstance*, a 68-page book of poems paired with imagery created in partnership with artist Roberta Smith, which achieved finalist status for the 2023 Colorado Book Award and the 2023 North Street Book Prize.

The poet wishes to express her gratitude to the Columbine Poets of Colorado and the NFSPS for awards and honors bestowed on the following poems: "Pillow Talk," "Wild Craft," "Flight School," "Thirst," "Poem to the Thief," "Pilgrim," "Last Rothko," and "Violets."

Most importantly, she extends her heartfelt thanks to all members of her widespread poetry family in Colorado, New Mexico, and California, although thanks are inadequate for what she has been given time and time again.

Contents

Agency	15
Letter to the Lineage of Women Poets	16
In the Dark	17
Thirst	18
True North	19
Wild Craft	20
Afterwards	21
Reservoir	23
Pillow Talk	24
A Private Wild	25
Spinster	26
Flight School	27
Truce	28
When Sorrow Lies Down on Top of Triumph	29
Origin Story	30
Another Theory of Relativity	33
Interior with Ida in a White Chair	34
Mastectomy	35
Origin of Patterns	36
Johnny	37
how the past retreats	38
Divination	39
Giverny	40
Starbucks	41
Apology	43
The Smoke Break	44
Poem to the Thief	45
that sharp snap?	46
Une Poire est une Femme	47
Patience	48
Scuppernong	49
Pandora's Query	51
Tips for Living in an Occupied Country	52

Jamais Vu	54
Revolution	55
Borscht	56
my dead ones,	58
Pilgrim	59
The Emigrants	60
Spell for Finding	61
the frost-covered leaves	62
The Bridge	63
Electricity	67
Tinsel Town	68
Night Vision	69
Violets	70
Home	71
napping	72
Joy	73
Coming of Age	74
Used, Rare, and Out-of-Print	76
An Old Soul Enters the Spirit World	77
a week later	79
Ebb	80
Last Rothko	81
Fault Lines	82
Blueprint	83
Finn	84
sit with me and listen	85
Absolution	86
A Light in the East	87
B e a s t	88
Other Love Poem	89
Continuum	90
Luminary	91

*Not knowing when the Dawn will come,
I open every Door,
Or has it Feathers like a Bird,
or Billows, like a Shore—*

—Emily Dickinson

Agency

Because the dirt road was shielded from the house,
the fields quieted from green to pale gold, the harvest in.

Because they thought she was in the sewing room upstairs,
like every morning.

Because she hid her legs in newly-stitched trousers,
stuffed her hair in a cap.

Because her heart was covered in love bruises.

Behind the jars of honey in the pantry was the spare pistol,
which she took.

Because she decided her story would begin with 'I'.

Letter to the Lineage of Women Poets

I do it because I must, and I would stop immediately if you told me you were bothered. So far I have been able to move silently behind you, collecting the scraps torn from the pages you carry as you wind your way through this thicket of brambles. I make loaves from what you discard, the words and phrases you assiduously cull from the brilliance that is your work. There are still abundant nutrients in what you reject. I've named myself your un-aproned and unpolished apprentice, constantly getting caught on briars as you move effortlessly through the tangle. Except for the night I saw you sink to the ground and weep, the page in your hand sodden with smeared letters, the way you ripped it into a hundred pieces. In disbelief, I watched from where I crouched. All that time I'd been certain you were blessed, possessed of a golden chalice filled with inspiration placed beside your bed every morning, and every morning you only had to drink. I approached and offered to take the splinters from your fingers after you'd buried the words you wanted no one to see. Together, we walked out of that place of thorns. You asked me if I wrote. I said I was about to start.

In the Dark

No request for an ID,
they recognize you instantly,
unlike a guard or militant sentry.

Outstretched arms invite
distant lights to speed sparkling
through their many fingers.

They do not know the language
of harm, their skill is to transmute
the air into a revivifying tonic

that grounds you, slows down
the turning of the great wheel,
reminds you why you live

outside of town,
under flaming stars
with a wisp of ice on the breeze,

in the presence and silence
of sycamore, willow, ash—
the trees.

Thirst

3, 4, 5 glasses of water gulped,
my phone ear hot and red
as we stir an eddy of kinship
to float and spin on.
Splashed by laughter,
quenched in the reliable
rainfall of each other's voices,
we ask, listen, tell, sigh.
No change in her husband,
sons striving in towns
where the decks are stacked
in opposite directions.
On my end a succession
of deaths, Mary's sacred heart
secreted behind my driver's
license, platitudes swept away
by a persistent graveyard wind.
In the shorthand of sisters
we commune and conspire,
we summon the family wellspring
to flood our parched acreages
and smother the sound
of the merciless clock.
We're back at home,
mapping the territory upstairs
and down, dodging the volcano,
paddling the rapids, vowing
not to let the other drown.

True North

You've rubbed your body against the trunks
of native oak and the sides of barns
tilting with decades of unrelenting usage.
You've tossed on a hotbed of obligations
and come away raw and scalded,
your skin shed between fallen logs
studded with moss and shelves of fungi.
A glance backward takes in eight years
of lost calves, favorite dog run over,
the relic of a first marriage punctuated
by tractors, hay bales, farm loans, barbed
wire, pheasants and badgers scuttling
in the underbrush. On your tongue is
the taste of rabbit stew, Amish butter,
wild raspberries rich with prickles, hosting
a throng of ticks. You've spoken of morels,
puffballs, pink bottoms, your grandmother
gone over thirty years, the home place
rife with ghosts, only curled photographs
left to salvage, and the compass in the
glovebox of your uncle's abandoned Merc.
Both feet on the threshold, the opening
frames you, naked. Let us hold each other
close these nights, and speak as little
as need be under the star-streaked sky.
Until you hold the compass again
in your workworn hands, take the map
laid out in mine with its own journeyed past.
Make room for me in your doorway.

Wild Craft

Woven from wood, a bowl, a cup,
a concavity sewn with no needle

or thread, a place of hiding
and warmth, shelter from the jaws,

claws and fangs of the underworld.
A sanctuary, tapestry of grass, wool,

hair, willow, reeds, sometimes
a bit of broken shell or colorless down

in the bottom, a small reference
to a recent arrival, a recent departure.

Placed high in the bowers of trees
or wedged in a niche on a vertical rock face,

these works are not for public viewing,
our winglessness reminding us

we are not meant to fly—trees, skies,
and mountaintops intended for those

more prepared to use them lightly,
leaving, at most, an empty nest behind.

Afterwards

When the world inside the small house started
its Sunday morning tilt after the memorial service
two days earlier, every room seemed a limp balloon
sighing in exhaustion against the tuneless chorus
of zipped-up overnight bags, car doors clunking,
choked goodbyes and long hugs on the crooked
Berkeley sidewalk, *love you, love you too, call us
later.* The confusion and comfort of tribal grief
were quickly replaced by a gravity-bound silence
that crept in like fog, overtaking the remaining three
who stared out the kitchen window at the floral
congregation staring back, a horde of banished
bouquets clustered on the rear porch and lower terrace.
They were uninvited guests doused in a collision
of fragrances, each florist's arrangement a colorless
still life with masses of virginal-looking flowers,
including those not ordinarily white that had been
forced to become so. They'd shown up at the door
in heady succession, guaranteed to gain entrance
after the shock of what had happened, the death
of a thirty-one-year-old son, the oldest of three.

Unsure of what to say, or never say, the last
visitor slipped through the screen door with grocery
bags and clippers to herd the assembly of flowers
to a remote table out of sight of the two inside.
She began to pull out stalks of leathery and feathery
ferns, clear plastic tridents used to spear miniature
condolence cards, crumbling chunks of hole-riddled
hard green foam. Wrist deep in a stew of tangled stems,
crushed petals and fetid water, she methodically culled
the pedestrian and exotic alike—enormous lilies

loaded with saffron-colored pollen that left stains
on arms scratched by prickly statice, spicy stock
entwined with carnations, spidery mums waving long
antenna-like fingers, and anemic anthuriums—all
tossed in the sack with no regrets. In stillness
the tulips appeared, solemn and pale, which she
placed one by one in a clear glass vase, ivory heads
bowing over the rim. With the crowd of elbowing
neighbors gone, spray after spray of orchids emerged,
faces turned outward in mute witness. Holding them
as one would an infant, she watched white return
to itself, a messenger from a distant land bearing
a small lantern, *blessings, blessings upon you.*
Inhaling the clean scent of an unusually silent
summer afternoon, she turned to the house,
cradling what she'd salvaged to light her way back.

Reservoir

The heart,
in addition
to blood, holds grief in store,
a task each chamber is often
used for.

Pillow Talk

Love, do you recall the starlings
billowing above the vineyards in winter?

How they filled the sky, their speckled
sails moving in endless undulance

more transfixing than the flash of fireworks,
that whoosh of wings a wanted sound,

thrilling and fearsome as Pacific
waves tall as office buildings

smashing the shore deeper
into the earth—divine pile driver,

oceanic sledgehammer—oh, those
noisome wonderful birds.

Can you tell me what perches in your mind
from our days in the west?

Write a couplet here,
starting at the base of my spine.

Let me feel each stroke of the first line
and let me lip read the rest.

A Private Wild

Could be a cove or a hollow,
easily overlooked by anyone else.
Something lives there,
something other than me.

I am a visitor, not a resident.
The something is untamed,
unpredictable.

Not exactly dangerous,
if I am attentive. In this private place
I will be attentive, therefore.

Wind carries the song of a tiny cricket,
joins the roar of a storm-swollen river.

Could be a dream state
or an alternate world, or both.

At times the challenge
is how to find the way in,
when to make my way out.

I'm unable to invite you,
because it is not mine.
Because it is wild. Private. Disobedient.

Miraculous.

Spinster

Wisdom arrives on strands so thin
we mistake it for spider's silk

until the cape is entirely spun
bringing an unmistakable warmth

to shoulders so recently bare
and shivering and innocent.

Flight School

At the workshop the poet pulled out a scalpel
to perform open heart surgery. I, for one,
didn't know I'd been hosting a colony of barnacles
until the inrush of oxygen converted them
to emeralds, orioles, and forgiveness. No one
bled or needed stitches, but we floated around
all day like jellyfish in love, every door inside us
flung open. For the first time in years some of us sang,
for the first time ever some of us swung our hips
in lusciousness ripe as Babcock peaches eaten straight
from the tree, while some of us wept aloud to taste
the nectar we'd cut out of our diets for a forgotten
reason long ago. When the poet slid the scalpel back
into its sheath and walked out into the night,
we hardly noticed how she lifted up like a great bird
and vanished into the darkness, so enchanted
were we with the sensation of wings sprouting
right from the place we were always told they would,
when we were children and believed in such things.

Truce

Last night
we spoke the truth,
suspended our sorrow.
Serenity arrived, briefly
borrowed.

When Sorrow Lies Down on Top of Triumph

How tough the gristle I chewed
for hours. Mashed it with my molars,
attempted to tenderize it with saliva,
got tired and tried to swallow.
Five times it stuck in my throat
to be chucked back up until I made
the phone call, said my answer was no,
explained why. I didn't acquiesce
to the explanation offered, stood
my ground, received their concession,
said thank you. The breeze of a small
victory filled the room. Ten minutes later
my husband called my name, beckoned me
to the back porch, said "Brownie's dead."
Our favorite girl, our trailblazing,
gate-jumping, quick study of a bird,
our finest hen. I sobbed as a child sobs,
with my head pushed into his body
to be absorbed, needing to obliterate myself
and my grief. I pressed so hard
the metal fasteners on his overalls
left imprints on my cheek.
The stand I'd taken, the inch I'd gained,
shrank to a handful of chaff,
worthless to all beings except Brownie,
who never encountered a batch of hay,
fresh or used, she could resist
sorting through like the champion
combine harvester she was,
until her inexplicable death
in the coop, where she lay limp
in a bed of thoroughly sifted straw.

Origin Story

The man who builds bridges for a living
strands all of his children on an island,
leaving them one rowboat and no life jackets.
He tells them he'll retrieve whoever survives
when they've matured and acquired
a greater degree of discernment and manners.
Because he has struck them often for infractions,
they stand silently in a row, still as statues.
Slow months of adjustment pass.
With the exception of typhoon season,
the children develop an afternoon habit
of gathering on the beach to compose and
practice a song with overlapping harmonies
and encyclopedic lyrics with close to ninety verses.
In the mornings, one girl trains to become
an endurance swimmer, another apprentices
as a lock picker, while the boys vie for top dog
at games of strategy conducted inside
labyrinthine structures made of seaweed.

In ten years the father returns. His children,
some now taller than he, line up on the sand
to sing him their song. The performance takes
several hours. After their voices deliver the final
heart-rending chorus, they laugh and spin in circles.
Silent tears stream down the father's face.
They smile and offer him food and drink
before they trap and truss him in braided lengths
of wakame which they use to strap his wrists
and ankles to the oarlocks. The swimmer
ties one end of a kelp rope around her waist
and the other to the rowboat in order to tow it
out to sea. Each kisses their father's forehead.

He glares back at them with the eyes of a hawk.
A mile offshore she cuts the rope. She reports
at last look his eyes were those of a vole.

More years pass. A helicopter lands to deposit
a woman who might be their mother.
The lock picker steps forward and asks
her intention. The woman wonders if they've
seen her husband, apparently gone missing.
She produces a photograph to pass around.
One brother volunteers "not lately."
She questions his word and wobbles off
in her city shoes to explore the island herself,
calling her husband's name. Holding
knives carved from shell, bark, and bone
they request permission to board the helicopter.
Seated and buckled in, they convince the pilot
to lift off. In synch with the powerful whipping
of the blades they sing their song one final time.

Similar to the variations of the sea that once
established their boundaries by defining certain
limits, assimilation on the continent is alternately
rough as a field of broken concrete, smooth
as the interior of a conch. Although an ephemeral
sense of exile is embedded in their psyches,
it is far milder than the acute ache of longing
for its birthplace exhibited by the song.
One day, with its lyrics, chords, and progressions
collected and collated, the song flies upward and
disappears, presumably to again climb prickly-
trunked trees, dash naked into the waves,
and ward off island ants huge as tarantulas.

Rumors are spread about the drifting scraps
of melody that have been said to emerge from
rooftop exhaust fans, or heard in the low hum
of a woman riding the early evening subway,
and once, in the unfurling of a thin viridian ribbon
from its roll in a florist's shop. An online search
for the song's composers is abandoned after every
database fails to uncover an accurate account
of their various names and aliases, or any other
verifiable facts. Although the song was never titled,
musicologists have dubbed it *The Chameleon Suite*.
Several have devoted their careers to capturing it
intact, as if it were an escaped prisoner, or an unruly
child in need of a lesson in acquiescence.

Another Theory of Relativity

Amidst wine spills and utility bills
the unseen taproot lies,
quietly lengthening
beneath a shared life.
When a foot trips on a woody knuckle
pushing through floorboards,
the breath catches in startlement,
as when a whale breaches vast water
right before our eyes,
magnificently dwarfing
the little tugboat
laden with all our concerns.

Interior with Ida in a White Chair

Vilhelm Hammershøi, 1900

She is facing the opposite direction.

She is mouthing a tune.

She is fingering a strand of beads.

She is cradling a bruise.

She is mending a tear in her dark dress.

She is staring at a spider climbing the table leg.

She is unfolding a piece of paper.

She is shelling peas into a blue bowl in her lap.

She is knotting a piece of string.

She is spinning two wheels of a child's toy.

She is examining a blister on her thumb.

She is sharpening the edge of a letter opener.

She is stilling her hands.

She is listening.

She will, in a moment, twist around to look behind her.

She knows she's been watched the entire time.

Mastectomy

Once upon a time a ravenous beast
begins feasting on the holy vessel of your life.

You conjure a tall woman extraordinarily skilled with a knife
to enter and evict by excision.

The evidence of that needful removal is an iron ring
of carvings that holds your torso in its grip.

This prevents you from exploding like a godhead,
or a grenade.

Stigmata on either side flow with fluid mistaken
by the neighborhood bear for the nectar of overripe fruit.

She swallows greedily, then curls her lip at the taste
of mending compound laced with blood.

A bright smear puddles on the floor
from liquid dripping off her jaw.

One day faint bird tracks will indicate
where the dunes once were.

There will be no need for an interpretive map.

Origin of Patterns

For a vicuña
a fall or injury
can impact
the integrity
of its wool,
a fact the spinner
will uncover.
Droughts
and floods
that hide in a tree
are only known
when it is felled,
the rounds of time
discovered.
An ache or wound
will lodge in cells,
seldom with full
consent, yet stinging
words bring back
the past to dim
our shining present.
To endure hurt
the heart must use
elaborate re-figurings,
forged less from
triumphs than the ruse
employed to secure
our moorings.

Johnny

Her name, the saying of it, brings the table
with its cloth back into the room, late afternoon
cards laid out in rows of solitaire, cigarette
balanced on the red enamel ashtray, coffee cup
off to the side, soon to be replaced by a glass
of ice cubes swimming in pale dry sherry.
She asks if I'm hungry, makes sure I've put
the kettle on, invites me to forage in the fridge
as she recites its contents, is happy when I sit
across her field of cards to listen and be listened to.
She lists what she'll have for supper, which movie
she's partway through, whether she'll stay up to see
the end, even though the story always sends her
sniffling to bed. If the weather's mild we move
to her tiny backyard garden, narrow as a hallway,
fragrant with jasmine cascading above pots
of white geraniums. *(They're really pelargoniums,
dear.)* We lower our voices to stop her neighbors
from hearing us agree and disagree about family
goings-on. She grabs the clippers to gather mint
for me to take home, asks if there's time to change
the darn furnace filter, hands me up the screwdriver
as she braces herself to catch me in her seventy-nine-
year-old arms if I topple off her extra-sturdy stepladder.
Calling *bye mama, see you later,* I let myself out
the screen door, careful not to slam it. Driving
home everything seems clear and uncomplicated.
If saying her name invites me in, the dilemma
is knowing the time to leave. Let the telephone
ring, let the rice boil over with a great hiss,
somebody please, snap your fingers, pull me
back to shore.

how the past retreats
inches of dust
on her death mask

Divination

Which line on your palm to heed
and which to ignore,

which Tarot card saves you
and which turns face down,

which star will blind
and which to wish on,

which fingers to lift in greeting
and which to keep crossed,

which smile to believe
and which hastens to leave?

From the dream of a lone shaman,
which road for the traveler,

for the fate of a midnight gambler,
which map for the mourner,

from the mind of an ancient scholar,
which bridge for the questioner,

for the sake of every lover
which life but this one, this one, *this one?*

Giverny

Later,
eyes turned cloudy,
the painter persisted,
finding a way to continue
anew.

His bridge—
wild nasturtiums,
a vast rambling garden,
lily pads hosting frogs at play—
Monet.

Starbucks

There was no other choice nearby, it had to be
Starbucks, which my nephew liked and I agreed
to settle for. We'd snuck away from a family get-
together so we could catch up for a few hours
before his flight back to California. I paid for our
cappuccinos, he bought a sandwich to eat on the plane.
Joe was a stunner, made you look twice, had those
sky-blue eyes that could skewer you to your seat.
Ninety minutes in he said there'd been someone,
but they fought over everything—brands of mayonnaise,
wet towels on the floor, how soon to switch lanes
before the disputed exit. They threw each other's clothes
out third floor windows, shouted midnight ultimatums,
got into a shoving bout in the courtyard at Ghirardelli
Square. He said if only they could live in a hut
in the woods with no phones, no nightclubs a taxi ride
away, no coke parties, no funsters down the hall.
I asked how they'd keep the big bad world from
showing up at the door. Locks! he grinned, dead bolts!
Said they'd do like you see in Westerns, sweep away
their footprints with a branch torn off a tree.
We laughed, stood to go.
                         Not seven weeks after
I drove him to the airport, his sandwich forgotten
on my back seat, he floated down a river with a bunch
of friends in inner tubes, and drowned. No life jacket.
Hearing the news bent my body in half. That night,
drunk, I transcribed a handful of Millay's death poems.
At the memorial I talked about Joe's eyes, how he
made you feel you were the only person on the planet
he was interested in. I nearly got through reading the poems
before my voice broke. Just about everyone had a story

they needed to tell. Joe's someone spoke near the end.
Thin, dark glasses, a little unsteady, knockout of a black
dress, stilettos. I wanted to go back to Starbucks, say Joe,
how about a hut sturdy enough to sit on a traffic island
in the middle of Market Street at rush hour, smack
in the center of all that holy confusion? How about
someone who can be with you *there,* because the world's
wise to you, it won't let you slink off to the backwoods,
merrily tearing branches off trees. That, and fifty other
pieces of advice were what I might have said, and he
might have listened to, had we been different people.
In the passenger drop-off lane, duffel in one hand,
he'd given me a tight one-armed hug, bird pecked me
on the lips, said how great we had a chance to talk.
Later, after I ate his sandwich, I texted him lunch
was on me next time.

Apology

Never having poured your kettle,
read your letters,
never having seen you fettered,
guessed your riddle,
been your brother or your sister
or your lover,
not once close by to still your shiver,
no mirror held to scry your future,
no songbird sent to bring you pleasure,
never having shown you whither,
how came I to call you bitter,
never having shared your weather?

The Smoke Break

Early summer in Seattle, the city of bounteous rain
euphorically drying out during a golden spell of sun
and heat, the two of them carrying bags of cashews
and almonds, sunflower seeds and pistachios,
lighthearted after sharing a bottle of wine in celebration
of her sudden midday decision to quit smoking.
He'd been waiting for her to liberate them from nicotine,
declaring his readiness any time she made up her mind,
fearing sabotage if he tried to go it alone. The wine
had been red, a color he preferred her not to drink,
saying her tongue turned dangerous, letting loose
a voice best kept caged, but they were so happy,
nearly giddy that day, like everyone else in Seattle.

On the walk home, swinging their sacks of salt
and crunch in the pale June evening, they laughed
about their strategy to occupy their mouths by eating
through the weekend into a new smoke-free life.
How it began or who said what could still be debated,
but in the span of four blocks nuts and seeds started
flying out of holes worn through the brown bags
as they flailed and swung them at each other,
high pitched shouts escalating in twilight despair,
the street and sidewalk pelted with roasted, salted
shrapnel. At last, empty and wrung out, they trailed
the limp shreds of paper the rest of the way, their
entire fortune left spent on the pavement. Cigarettes
and lighters came out of exile the moment the front
door closed. They pulled their smokescreens down
around them like shawls, as night finally descended.

Poem to the Thief

The paintings were hung in the library,
where everyone is unequivocally welcome.
When it was discovered you took not one,

but two, and stashed the frames behind
a radiator, your theft wasn't reported right away
in the hope it was a prank with a happy ending.

They haven't been recovered, something
you already know. Because of what you did,
this is what I want: that your room was spare,

the light dim, your life lacking, the way forward
unclear. You knew separateness was overcoming you,
and were desperate for illumination,

desperate for an unnameable thing,
straining to reach the rope beauty tosses
that could lift you out of an encroaching blindness.

I want your possession of the paintings
to change your direction and beget a monumental
shift. And, before you proceed into your new life,

I want you to write the artist to tell her what she has
unknowingly given you, and how you fully understand
what is now owed. You do not need to sign your name.

that sharp snap?
an angelic heart breaking
along the old fracture

Une Poire est une Femme

One day the weapons held in certain eyes that devour
women with a hunter's gaze will be disarmed.

Until then, we ask for shelter in the sanctuary of pear.
Upright or half-reclined, the wordless dignity inherent

in pear-ness is maintained, even after the bite, the swallow,
the disappearance, as want transmutes into tenderness.

Untroubled by hunger's gaze, ripened by the sun,
revered by young children, paid homage by imagists,

praised by Madame DuClaire who shared slices of *clafoutis*
with her *confrères,* a pear is central to a kitchen god's prayer.

Pink-blushed, pale yellow, saturated in crimson, tall,
squat, rust-dusted brown, golden-hued, green-limned,

slender, elegant, rotund, creamy, firm, fragrant,
in the company of pears nothing compares.

Look for us there.

Patience

with a bow to WC Williams

So much depends
on the short red hydrant

huddled in the snow
ready for smoke and smolder

even in this interval
of cold white skin

worn by a world
so hot at its core.

Scuppernong

Slabs of watermelon, unlikely things suspended in Jello,
wheel-chaired grandmother, saggy-diapered babies,
Miracle Whip coleslaw, ham so salty you needed
a quart chaser of sweet tea, voices swarming: *hey,
how you? Fill that plate, girl, don't be shy now.*
His family's annual get-together tended to wind him
up in a manic way familiar to her, a good time to be
extra careful in everything she said and did. No matter
who or what he was they welcomed him home,
like families do, and that included her, even though
they still hadn't gotten married. After three hours
of chewing and joking he signaled he was overdue
for a breather. They drove down an easy-to-miss dirt lane
through swampy lowland to the fishing 'cabin,'
a single-wide trailer squatting like a toad in a patch
of scrubby woods. Every time they'd been there
she sensed a crime just itching to happen. Grayish
tilting floor, corner to corner fug of mildew, every
doorway a tad too low, one lone hornet bigger than
a gorilla's thumb droning loud as a surveillance plane
at the window screen. Last time he'd twisted her arm,
left marks after she said something that didn't sit right.
Time before that, she'd found a musty kimono in a drawer,
put it on to see if the faded flowered silk made her feel
like someone else, until he called her by his second wife's
name on purpose. They rummaged around in the cupboards
for creamer and instant coffee, crammed behind cans
of greens and black-eyed peas. She said tell you what,
I'll go get us a giant bowl of that peach ice cream
your dad was about to make, why don't you boil the water,
rinse two cups, see me back here in a sec. He said nope,
I'm coming too. She said well, I'll have to spill your Aunt

June's secret, she's holding onto some birthday present
for you she needs me to squirrel down here, you can't
let on I said anything, and you'd best not come or she'll
shoot me her squinty-eyed daggers. He said dammit
girl, then don't dawdle, I've got my eye on the clock,
and don't be bringing us any of that scuppernong wine
Jimmy and Lorraine think is so special, tastes like
cough medicine gone bad. She figured he'd follow
her out to the car with some last-minute warning,
but he just stood in the doorway, stone-faced.
She stopped at the intersection where the lane met
the paved road. Charlotte was to the left, the Atlantic
five, six hours east of that. To the right, the mountains.
From there it was a straight shot west to the high desert
she once tore herself away from. A drumbeat in her chest
picked up. She eased her foot back on the gas pedal,
wondered if she was ready to feel like someone else,
curious if she'd like that person any better.

Pandora's Query

Do you have one too,
a container for all
that lives unsaid in you?

Tips for Living in an Occupied Country

1.
Apprehend the difference
between the smell of a
snake, the smell of a rat,
and that of a chameleon.

2.
Keep an eye out for what
is palmed in the ruling
party's handshake,
swaddled in the translucent
gauze of camaraderie.

3.
When your voice is targeted,
note which words conceal
shrapnel. Passing remarks
are timed to weather up
months or years later.
Mind they miss your heart
and other vitals on their
jagged way out.

4.
Expect to be treated as
unglazed clay, porous
and receptive. Exhibit
no anger. The legal
tender allowed our kind
is cosseting. Apply in
small increments when
deemed unavoidable.

5.
Arrange your apothecary
with cunning. The agéd
regime's phobias and
unhealed wounds foment
abnormal cravings
for the salty and sweet.

6.
Whosoever asks to break
bread with you, examine
the configuration of
the tongue for a forked
appearance, observe what
is spread upon its surface.

7.
Use one apprenticeship
as a cover for the other
one.

8.
Smuggle your real work to
a free country. There are
more of us than you know,
ears to the same ground.

*undated flyer found
in a crawl space*

Jamais Vu

Can white be an absence
or a presence,
and then, is grey
silver's disguise?

There's a young girl in a room
believing what she wants
is too far away
because she's unable to picture it.

What is the opposite
of lightning
if not
the unseeing stare?

Lend her these eyes
that have leapt across
several kinds
of distance.

What happiness
to sit awhile in darkness.

Revolution

When watched
he doesn't move,

similar to the planets
and certain types of clouds.

A later glance out the window
finds him in a new spot, as does a third look.

At last it becomes clear
that they move in a slow dance,

the sun partner to the cat,
their duet circumscribed by shadow,

a private communion while the earth spins
around its stunning emperor of fire.

Borscht

O clear ruby mirror
still as a reposing lake,
your cool round face
reflects the stain of history

Those drifting slivers of beet in the bottom of my bowl
move like ceaseless goldfish, or sharks slowly circling
a meal. Onto the surface is plopped sour cream,
a white island the color of refuge, of surrender, of ash
and bone shoveled out of crematoria in three countries,
or was it five? A beautiful magenta results.

soup of steppes, soup of shtetlach

How often we find it served cold, as is served the revenge
of continuance on the plate of the world. Its liquid nature
has not extinguished the hot needle of fact that sears the truth
onto flesh, memory, paper, granite and marble, cattle cars
camouflaged with graffiti.

soup of yellow stars, soup of ghettos

As I commence to eat, reflected in the curve of my spoon
are faces shadowed with recognition. One sees the failure
of perception, another the inability to escape, and yet another
the impossibility of forging belief into survival.

soup of the disappeared, soup of the camps

When the mass graves were dug, even then the roots
of beets fattened in a neighboring plot of dirt, witness
to the great cloud of sky-bound spirits destined
to circle the earth in perpetuity. If those who have been
exterminated do not perish absolutely, do they endure
through inextinguishable truth and remembrance alone?

O clear ruby mirror
still as a reposing lake,
in you we taste
the soup of the irredeemable

my dead ones,
is that you whispering,
or the trees, or both?

Pilgrim

At the wailing wall
in Jerusalem

she crawled to touch
God's ragged hem,

was welcomed home
after long travails,

a rootless time
of odds and ends.

From deep inside
her chambered heart

a rush of prayers
came out of hiding,

absorbed in stone
like a holy sponge

of acceptance and abiding.

The Emigrants

Here, we are nowhere
we have walked before.

Save for the scouring wind
the surround is soundless bedrock.

Oceans, prairies, cities of the past
lie east and west at a vast remove,

no ancestral thumb
presses down.

A blank slate
welcomes the strangers,

beckons us through
the unbound gate.

Spell for Finding

Up the seer's left sleeve hides your sealed request,
In the forest undressed leaves dervish unswept,

> *no chore without heft,*
> *no weave without weft,*
> *the first step of all quests*
> *is half-choice, half-guess*

Grief leads to theft of salt the muse wept,
Melts into darkness beneath trees full of nests,

> *if bereaved is bereft*
> *to adapt is adept,*
> *what is apt is belief*
> *in the context of yes*

Sleep plumbs the depths where cleave seeks out cleft,
Moon eases east-west to illumine your rest,

> *beyond the last dream*
> *through the door of perchance*
> *a seam opens up*
> *to reveal the entranced*

Veiled in a drift of burning frankincense
Lie the unmapped lands of your heart's seventh sense,
Read the clue in your breast, take the step that's the next,
Lest the heft of the test rends the mesh of the quest.

the frost-covered leaves
do they remember
how green they were in spring?

The Bridge

The villagers referred to our hermitages
as barnacles because of the way each
clung to the steep mountainside.
My kitchen window faced that of a woman
named Clara. Our night candles flickered
in signals that touched but didn't pierce
the membrane of our intentional solitude.
To invite a deep tranquility that encouraged
the mind away from the external,
our contemplation rooms were placed
on the north side where the outlook
was nearly all sky.

A foot bridge spanning the 1400' drop
was suspended between us: rope strung
through slats of wood with a cleverly knotted
handrail to keep one upright in the unceasing sway.
Before the commencement of our meditation
retreats we spent a month in intensive training
on how to repair the bridge, which required
constant monitoring and upkeep.
There was visible sloppiness in the repairs
of past retreatants, in the way a secondhand
sweater reflects the carelessness of a previous
wearer who used the wrong color of thread
to mend it with uneven hasty stitches.
Clara and I agreed to methodically replace
every slat and length of rope over our five
years of residency.

We were permitted to visit each other
for two hours every forty-three days,
a gift of occasional companionship.
Because our palms bloomed with calluses,
our fingers studded with wood slivers,
in the scant hours together we'd bend
over each others' hands to apply salves,
wield tweezers, and hum in overtones
that filled the small room where we sat.
We always shared a meal, savoring
what the other had prepared from
the limited ingredients provided.
Our communion expanded with every
two-hour session spent together.
Talk centered on winter storms, bridge
repairs, the taste of what we were eating.
We'd been asked to wait for the yearly visits
from our individual teachers to discuss
any concerns or questions we might have
about our ongoing retreat practice.
The wish to be in her company rivaled
my dependence on the sun and moon
as constants. I made a calendar with rows
of X's up to the days of our meetings,
highlighted in brilliant yellow. There were
mornings I awoke sobbing from nightmares
in which the bridge had been torn in half.

On visitation day I prostrated myself
in tongue-tied humility. My teacher said,
"Rise, let us sit across from each other."
Her eyes shifted to the calendar on the wall.
She unhooked it and asked me to tell her
what the marks signified. After I explained
she sat silently with eyes closed until ready
to speak again. She said there was no woman
in a hermitage on the facing mountain,
and there was no bridge. Her words paralyzed
me. I was incapable of looking outside to
prove her wrong, terrified to see if she was right.
She instructed me to devote the next year
to building a different bridge, an inner one
to the unknowable infinite, unhindered
by the distraction of an auxiliary sun or moon.

There is nothing else to say about the ensuing
four years or the completion of my retreat.
I was rendered a clumsy tightrope walker
by my lengthy re-entry into the external world
as I strove to retain the sense of the inner bridge
I'd struggled to construct. To achieve a reliable
balance between interaction and indwelling,
work and rest, relationships and solitude,
was more of a challenge than I'd ever anticipated.
The process was exhausting. Surprisingly simple

things restored me, like perfectly brewed oolong
in a quiet café. On a drear drizzly day I ducked
into an unfamiliar coffeehouse and ordered tea.
It was then I saw Clara, seated in a corner, writing
in a notebook. Everything inside me—my bearings,
my words, assumptions, beliefs—collapsed.
I had little control over the clatter of the cup
and saucer in my hand or the vein throbbing
in my throat. I half feared, half hoped a seam
would open in the floor to drop me into safety
and darkness. As one does on a bridge swaying
in a fierce wind, I moved slowly toward her,
my eyes trained from long practice to catch
the precise moment when she would notice
footsteps approaching, and lift her head to look.

Electricity

Gradually subsumed

in dusk's deepening blue,

immense eastern clouds

illumined by a series of lightning flashes

reflect bursts of glowing pink

limned with silver,

reminding us of a woman

we once glimpsed in the window

of a darkened room

as she stood unmoving in a pale satin slip,

briefly phosphorescent

in our passing headlights.

Tinsel Town

In tandem with the season of resurrection
        comes a timely explosion of blossoms

in dreamlike mists of lavender, periwinkle,
        and the blue-violet of vintage perfume bottles,

found in select neighborhoods overlaid with blankets
        of petals in a palette capable of transporting one

to a place of entrancement, where hearts braced for
        discouragement fall prey to the uplift of magic in the air,

underfoot, and laced through the hair, a land where
        movies simmer and stew and the unlikely comes true

in Los Angeles when the jacarandas bloom,
        causing hopes to renew on the cross-town drive

                to the audition room.

Night Vision

Out the windows hay-colored
hills concealed an ocean
that sent a breeze of salt
to wash over their skin.
Rows of eucalyptus stretched
to scrape the blue ceiling of sky.
They had no cause for words
in the first house.

In the second house
they heard cats speak in tongues,
calves call to their mothers
in the field next door.
Under the shade of wild grapevines
busy knitting a second roof
to cover the first one,
they began to learn each other's
language in fragments of phrases.

By the time of the third house
they had become bilingual,
had discovered how to find
the opening to presence
and the door to silence
even in the dark,
the rooms where they ate and slept
connected by game trails.

In the tunnel of night
coyotes shared prophecies
of a fourth house with no location,
although their keen voices
pointed to the constellations
for the duration of their song.

Violets

My terminally modest mother and I were sitting
outside at her house, speaking the language of flowers.
We mooned over nuances of color, scents both subtle
and soporific, the magnificent variety of petals.
All references to pollination, sex organs and plant
propagation were carefully avoided. I mentioned
how I looked forward to a coastal drive in late summer
to see the naked ladies. She gasped and shrieked
my name so loudly Faye next door came running
over. I tried not to laugh as I explained how
the glossy green leaves shoot up in spring, but
the fragrant pink lilies bide their time until August,
when they suddenly appear on tall bare stems
in clusters by the roadside. A few in a Mason jar
will fill the room with a delicate sweetness.
From then on, my mother skirted the common name
I'd used, preferring the Latin, *Amaryllis Belladonna,*
which carries a different innuendo. In the moments
before she was cremated, I tucked a small bunch
of violets into her blouse. She'd been so pleased
when she discovered them growing in my messy yard.
Violets carry multiple meanings in the language
of flowers, modesty being one, innocence
another. The most obvious and timeworn is love,
which is what I wanted to send with her into
the unknown, trusting she'd find a garden waiting.

Home

Where I live is where I fit
and that is you.

Under your wing
inside your warmth

I come to rest and rid myself
of the chill and sorrow

that faithfully visit
in the in-between hours of dusk

when the arms of the past
reach for the vulnerable.

There's a silence in you
where I go to pray

away from the noise of myself.
How this happened I do not know—

you anchored, constant—
me, darting in the air like a fugitive kite.

What runs in you is deep and clear.
I drop my cup and drink and drink.

When they ask my address
I say your name out loud.

napping
in the arms
of my mother's couch

Joy

Let the brush follow
the contour of a hill
and begin the story of clouds
traveling across the day.

Use Raw Umber,
Ultramarine Blue.
Mix Payne's Gray, *Terre Verte,*
dot the distance with dark shapes
defined enough to say "trees,"
but not what kind.

Hint at a fence,
Raw Umber again,
Mars Violet in the shadows,
Burnt Sienna placed sparingly
for dimension.

Notice the colors you favor,
be curious about the ones you shy from.
Each pigment is a language,
each stroke speaks of your practice.

Stroll, don't gallop,
let your heart slow.
At the center of all there is
is a lantern glowing.

Gamboge. Naples Yellow.
There is no finish line.

Coming of Age

with a line from Denise Levertov

In a land made iridescent gold by radiant light
shimmering across a valley circled by dark mountains,
the compound stood in crystalline air under a flashing sky.

In her private corner on the roof where she'd crept
well before noon, the girl drew and painted on small crisp sheets
borrowed from a desk with a rudimentary lock.

An unusual sound prompted her to glance up from her drawing
in time to see a tiger streaking through the courtyard.
She watched each muscular leap as it vaulted over walls

without stopping, until the blur of stripes melted into a waver
on the northern horizon. The scent of tiger drifted and settled like
a heavy mist. The horses and hounds paced, moaning, fitful.

Two seasons would pass before the hens resumed laying.
Having once glimpsed the inside of a room holding racks of guns,
the girl understood the enormous danger the animal had risked

to bring her a message. She apprenticed herself to the task of
becoming worthy of what she'd been given. She sketched curves,
the shape of a head, practiced the depiction of agility and grace

without the use of color as distraction. Color would come later,
a prize to be bestowed when she had made her many preparations
for the tiger's return. A dream assured her no one would see them

if they left at dawn, signaled by a mockingbird singing the song
of a thrush. She knew to burn her cache of drawings and paintings
beforehand, bury the ashes, cut her waist-length hair.

In a land made bright with luminescence
eyes flash with primordial prescience
Come, come, into animal presence

Used, Rare, and Out-of-Print

in homage to Treehorn Books, Brodsky Bookshop, Books of Interest, Moby Dickens, Cody's, Moe's, Black Oak Books, Shakespeare & Co, Green Apple Books, City Lights, Dutton's, Changing Hands, Lithic Bookstore, The Tattered Cover, Levin & Co, and a multitude of others

No incense in this temple
redolent of must from a past tense,

a populace of selves on dense, dark shelves.

Dust motes flourish, cells turn porous,
my spirit commences to genuflect.

Like a bee feigning aimlessness
I wander freely in timelessness,

immersed in possibility, adrift in camaraderie.

The retrieved, the next, the almost forgotten,
reside inside these covers,

an infinite reserve of eloquent lovers.

An Old Soul Enters the Spirit World

In the back forty of her closet hung a prophet's
velvet coat, seldom worn but we knew it was there,
beyond the scarves she wrapped twice around her throat,
crowned by a mist of long silver hair. A blizzard,
she recalled, came to her christening, where seven
wizards conferred about her upbringing, Montana
never stopped whispering in her train case of mysteries.

Black widows convened in her medicine bag garage,
mountain raspberries sweetened her memory's tongue,
a lighter clicked, an inch of ash flicked, her kookaburra
laugh pinballed deep in her lungs. Her left ankle was tattooed
with the clank of shackles, hooked to past lives towing
the usual regrets, she was regularly seen with her entourage
of grackles, wreathed in the smoke of nine thousand cigarettes.
Hawks levitated in feathered respect when she gazed
with her blue-eyed prescient stare, they understood her
consecrated fear of the shamanic grizzly bear. Befriended
by neighboring geese and squirrels, she collaged her
visions with corvine chuckle, fox slink, mouse blink,
and the parliament of birds in her parallel worlds.

Her heart she kept close, forged from miner's gold,
steel-cased in a pearlescent shell, camouflaged most days
by a fortress of twigs, bound tightly by hand to fortify
the maze that concealed the depth of her wisdom well.
Folded in the niches of her soul's house of wishes
were the lines she wrote for few to see, on pages scribed
in coal black ink. At times she lost them, or misplaced
them somewhere under the laundry sink. Our Rachel
found them, dried and ironed them, gave us solace
in a river of poems from which we drink, while from

her perch the old soul winks. Her tribe set their nets
to catch the words that flew wild when she died—
in ceremonies of trance and chant, in rituals of
dreamlike dance, on thresholds of holy happenstance.
Down low we bow to honor her in verse, summoning
the chimes of the Multiverse to exalt in the glory of
one who rhymed with Story, possessed of her share
of alternate names, but I just called her Laurie James.

a week later
her long hair
on my beret

Ebb

Memory fled with an odd-shaped sack,
hauling all it learned
strapped to its back.

Purpose drifted off,
adjourned from sight,
lost in smoke as it burned mid-flight.

Color faded to cellophane,
no blush discerned on a bleached terrain,
no trace of errant pigment stains.

Language spurned us when it left—
we cupped our ears to catch a word,
forgetting we'd turned deaf.

Though the gate was unlatched
the heart yearned to stay, its company
the comfort of a tarnished watch.

As the peripheral diminishes,
desire puts down the empty glass,
pays the wage old age has earned,
strips patina off its finishes.

Last Rothko

Suppose it was a late hour, his face in the black studio windows only able to glimpse half of itself. Suppose he ignored the phone, then left the receiver off, as obelisks of smoke rose from scattered ashtrays. His wife estranged, daughter distant, the work was priced high, no one to witness what was being painted towards. Or maybe it was 6:30, 7 a.m., when the cold rooms began to smolder in pale gray light, an acrid weave of sweat, turpentine, and solitude hovering. Even though the coffee tasted bitter with cream close to sour, he kept drinking it against a muffled soundtrack of early sirens, trucks, and taxis. What it wasn't was midday, the brief buoyant moment, city on its slow axis turning to afternoon, lunch being gotten, rattling keys of the postman sending a faint lyric up from the street. That's when the sense of momentum exploded with an overarching obligation to lay down the layers with a depth plumbed by perseverance, edged with absence, and possibly the weekend would be fair and milder as promised.

Fault Lines

Although we might not
mark the first crack,
it's far more likely
we'll note the second—
a slow widening
of what was once
quite solid, until
the result must be
termed a gap.
Caulk, putty, mortar,
glue, some of it works,
some of it won't,
depending on surface,
tilt, and substance,
the unknown quotient
of unknown quirks.
Unless it's a friendship
pulling apart,
as a glacier glides
through the polar ocean—
leaving us frozen,
words at our feet,
like wounded birds
with a song unspoken,
unable to mend
a wing that's broken.

Blueprint

House with Vault of Skull
Window of Eye, Floor of Bone

oh my hammer, my chisel, my whistle, my shadow

Refuge with Fountain of Blood
Wall of Skin, Current of Breath

oh my clockworks, my sump pump, my pup tent, my echo

Shelter with Ridge of Spine
Door of Mouth, Ceiling of Sinew

oh my mule, my chassis, my paradox, my yes and no

Armature with Beams of Tendons
Terrain of Muscle, Parade of Cells

oh my library, my camel, my coffin, my minstrel show

Periscope, Colony, Metaphor of More and Less
Temporary Geography
Temple of Biology

oh my crucible, my chalice

first friend, last foe

Finn

9/11/2004–8/14/21

Having used his name
to swim away from everything
familiar, he's a fish
under the surface now,
learning to glide in fluidity.
Freed from a hard-packed
earthen path, distanced
from the too-bright scrutiny
of an unfiltered sun,
he drifts with ease
in the deep currents.
Gills and iridescent scales
begin to grow,
his undulations churn the sand
where shards of shells
mixed with bits of bones
have accumulated.
A tail emerges as rudder
to steer him to the start
of the next story.
Because he can no longer speak
to those on dry land
who hold a vigil in his name,
he asks the water to speak for him
by offering consolation on its waves,
inside the rain,
in the stillness of lakes.
How trusting he is to believe
his message will be heard,
even over the thunder
of the waterfall.

sit with me and listen
to all the pins of the world
dropping

Absolution

When your throat is lined
with new confessions
blocked by fear of repercussions

Take a detour up the spiral stairs
through dark inner ear
and tarpit of tears

To the topmost floor
of utter vision
beyond the angst

Above the friction
standing with one arm
tied at your back

With dreams surviving
a diet of lack
on the south wind is chance

Flying with hawks
in the field hope embodied as fox
study clouds as language

Survey the plains
burn the chokeweed
float on the flames

A Light in the East

Mystic sister, you turned solitude
into a pyre on which convention writhed—

after the old alphabet burned
you replaced it with your finer glyphs,

wondrous to those who've felt
the terrifying quake of lift—

Emily, you detonate chills in me,
a woman who stumbles to glimpse

the Transcendence you see,
you with your flies and occasional Bee—

—who stands resolute
in the Lineage of Possibility—

B e a s t

In the first months after surgery an elephant's trunk
lightly skimmed the surface of my body,
roaming in search of breasts disappeared overnight.

Neither a nipple-seeking infant nor a lover's slow hand,
it was an orienteer's instrument calibrated to establish context
in a new unmapped topography.

These days the trunk curls around my torso,
quietly alert to shifts in air flow, corner-of-the-eye stirrings,
whiffs of scent captured by large finely tuned nostrils.

Whatever advances is unseen, inching through jungle, deep water,
cellular pathways, etheric channels. A predawn whisper questions
whether the timer has already been set to signal my last hour.

My animal stands, flaps her massive ears, knocks
the ticking nuisance aside with her steamroller of a foot.
She trumpets in a major key before her mouth opens wide

for pears, handfuls of toasted walnuts, jam-laden black figs.
This is what matters. I peel a mango, her favorite, lick the sticky
pulp off my fingers. She sways and rumbles in anticipation.

This is *all* that matters.

Other Love Poem

She was shoreline. He was pasture.

She traced wild yeast. He, mycelium.

He was owl. She, skink.

She pleated a cloud.
He scribed a parallelogram.

He was pause. She was *sotto voce*.

She wore fog. He, lightning.

She was crossroad. He was axle.

He had been mica.
She once was moss.

She spun. He strode.

She was his constancy. He, her galaxy.

Her collarbone, his fulcrum.

His blood, her river.

Continuum

On the day life was frozen in the shape
of an igloo I shrank to the size of a rabbit
crouched beneath a bush, white-furred

like the blind wolf who tracked me by scent,
the one presently snuffling with her probe of a nose,
which inspires me to write these requests:

let the eulogy proclaim my eyes at the last were
calm and wise, my face a visage of peace and acceptance
with not one discernible speck of resistance;

say I died with a lungful of air to propel me skyward
above the earth, where I looked down with compassion
and sorrow at the astonishing smallness of it;

tell how I discovered the shape of time to be like a sunburst
or exploding star, how being astride the gyroscopic wonder of it
I was no longer confined or constrained;

let it be known I will be wearing the face I had
before my parents were born, ready to identify myself
when you arrive to join me.

Luminary

Begin again brightly
says my friend of the moon,
slip through the water
getting wet only slightly
without drenching the hem,
the bread or the psalter.
Go slowly but spritely,
find the path to the altar,
hear the doves at the font
before evening turns nightly,
when dreamers find a heaven
to be healed of their want,
where all are met kindly
with the words *travel lightly*.

About the Author

Barbara Ford writes poems in longhand, sitting in a striped chair that was once in the lobby of the Broadmoor Hotel in Colorado Springs. Soon after moving from the West Coast in 2005, she began reading poetry over the air at the Salida community radio station KHEN. Eight months later she inaugurated *Poets and Minstrels,* a weekly radio hour now in its twentieth year of offering contemporary, cross-cultural, and classical poetry to her listening audience.

Her poetry chapbook *Once Familiar* was published in 2016 by Finishing Line Press. Her 2022 collaboration with visual artist Roberta Smith, *In Pursuit of Happenstance,* a pairing of poetry and imagery, achieved finalist status in both the 2023 Colorado Book Awards and the 2023 North Street Book Prize. Barbara has presented her poetry at festivals and conferences throughout the state, and her poems have been published in various print and online journals, magazines, and anthologies.

Under the migration path of sandhill cranes, she lives with her husband Terry Orchard and a flock of backyard chickens in the crosswinds of two mountain passes in southwestern Colorado, where the prevailing night sounds are the call and response of coyotes, the sway of cottonwoods, and the Morse code of owls.

www.ingramcontent.com/pod-product-compliance
Lightning Source LLC
Chambersburg PA
CBHW031200160426
43193CB00008B/459